WHO AM I?

What It Means to Be Made in the Image of God

Christopher Klofft, S.T.D.

Pflaum Publishing Group
A division of bayard

ABOUT THE AUTHOR

Christopher Klofft is Associate Professor of Theology at Assumption University in Worcester, Massachusetts. He is a moral theologian, specializing in the areas of marriage and family, as well as the rapidly changing fields of sexuality and bioethics. He also has a specific interest in the intersection between theology, spirituality, and popular culture, reflecting on the ways in which we can find God in unusual places. Of particular note is his love for superheroes as morality tales for the modern era. He is the author of *Living the Love Story: Catholic Morality in the Modern World* and *God-Like: Sexuality and the Image of God*. He lives in Worcester with his wife and two sons.

The Subcommittee on the Catechism, United States Conference of Catholic Bishops, has found this text, copyright 2025, to be in conformity with the *Catechism of the Catholic Church*.

Imprimatur: +Most Reverend Robert J. McManus, S.T.D., Bishop of Worcester, December 5, 2024

Written by Christopher P. Klofft, S.T.D.
Edited by David Dziena
Designed by Jennifer Poferl

Cover image: Prostock-studio/stock.adobe.com, Natalya Natalia/stock.adobe.com, Sedyakina/stock.adobe.com.
Images: top of pages: Natalia Sedyakina/stock.adobe.com; page 11: Renáta Sedmáková/images.adobe.com, Franco Origlia/Contributor/Getty, Vatican Pool/Contributor/Getty; page 14: GiorgioMorara/stock.adobe.com; page 16: Petrik/stock.adobe.com; page 18: EKH-Pictures/stock.adobe.com; page 21: fizkes/stock.adobe.com; page 24: Lightfield Studios/stock.adobe.com; page 29: PKpix/stock.adobe.com; page 31: Natalya/stock.adobe.com; page 35: Drobot Dean/stock.adobe.com; page 37: Prostock-studio/stock.adobe.com; page 40: Johannes Joas; cropped & shifted by Rabanus Flavus.

Pflaum Publishing Group
500 Salisbury Street
Worcester, MA 01609
800-543-4383
pflaum.com

FSC-STD-50-001

ISBN: 978-0-89837-002-7
PGW-5606
Printed in the U.S.A.

bayard

MIX
Paper | Supporting responsible forestry
FSC® C005010
FSC
www.fsc.org

CONTENTS

INTRODUCTION

CCC, 2074: "When we believe in Jesus Christ, partake of his mysteries, and keep his commandments, the Savior himself comes to love, in us, his Father and his brethren, our Father and our brethren. His person becomes, through the Spirit, the living and interior rule of our activity."

How do we live as faithful Catholics in a confusing world?

There's no question that trying to be a faithful Catholic in the world today can be a real challenge. Often, it seems that the teaching proposed by the Church is not just different from the wider culture around us, but also out of touch. Even for people who take their Catholic faith seriously, it's really easy to dismiss the harder parts of Catholic morality as something that made sense "back then" but that has to change to fit into the world we live in today.

Of course, the Church's teaching comes from God himself, revealed through the Bible and the lived experience of the Christian community throughout history. Human beings didn't suddenly become different creatures ten, fifty, or a hundred years ago. The teaching that led Christians before us to happiness with Christ in this life now and in Heaven for eternity still applies to us. Instead of focusing on difficult "rules" we have to follow, this booklet is going to look at some of the challenging parts of Catholic teaching so we can see why it is important and why we should do our very best to be the kind of people God made us to be.

WHO AM I?

CCC 357: "Being in the image of God the human individual possesses the dignity of a person, who is not just something, but someone. He is capable of self-knowledge, of self-possession and of freely giving himself and entering into communion with other persons."

What it means to be made in the Image of God

Before we can ever know how we should live our lives, we have to know who we are. The kind of person I am leads to the kind of choices I make. If I'm a person who cares about others, thinks of them lovingly and respectfully, and takes responsibility for my choices, I am likely to act in a way that is loving and respectful of others and myself. The choices I make, the things I do, and the feelings I have about my actions also shape who I am as a person.

When we think about the kind of person we are, however, where do we begin? Every one of us has a lot of "facts" that we could say about ourselves: "I come from this place, I belong to this family, I like this kind of music, I belong to this church." But despite all these different facts, there is really one that is most important of all: I am created by God to be like God. I am loved by God and I am called to love like God loves.

All the other facts we can say about ourselves have varying degrees of importance. For example, who your family members are is more important than your favorite flavor of ice cream! But none of those facts compares to the fundamental truth that you were created by God in is own image, to love as he loves.

The Book of Genesis says, “God created mankind in his image, in the image of God he created them; male and female he created them” (1:27). This verse tells us not only that we were made by God, but that we were made to be *like* God. We can do the things that God can do, and nothing else God created on earth can do the same. Furthermore, each one of us is unique—special in the whole history of the universe!

What does this mean exactly? It means four things. First, we can think and understand; we can look at the world around us and learn about it. We can also think about things we can't see with our eyes, like love and math and literature. Second, we're not just driven by instincts like a dog, or a bird, or any other creature; we can make reasoned choices. Third, we can create. This can take all sorts of forms, such as art and music, but one of the most important forms of creation we can engage in is when husband and wife participate with God in bringing forth a new God-like human being: a baby! Finally, we can love. God's love is so powerful that he can create and heal with just a word. He invites us to share in that love so we too can bring joy, healing, and peace to the world around us.

Name some choices you make every day.

____

____

____

____

Everything else we are has to be compared to the truth that we are made in God's image. Anything about ourselves that helps us to live God's love more fully is good; anything about ourselves that makes it harder to love truthfully is something we should strive, with God's help, to remove from our lives.

Because God himself is a relationship—remember God is Father, Son, and Holy Spirit in one God—he made us to be in relationships also. We come to truly know who we are in our loving and truthful relationships with God and others. None of us is meant to make it through life on our own. We are in this together, as a community, as a Church.

Throughout the rest of this book, we're going to see what it means to live as people made in God's image, made to love truthfully in relationship with God and one another. Before we get to some of the issues that face us today, though, let's take a moment to talk about the relationship between faith and science.

SUMMARY

- Who we are determines what kinds of actions we take.
- Each of us is made in the Image of God.
- This means we can think, choose, create, and love as God does.
- God calls us to be in loving and truthful relationships with him and with one another.

FAITH AND SCIENCE

CCC, 159: "Though faith is above reason, there can never be any real discrepancy between faith and reason. Since the same God who reveals mysteries and infuses faith has bestowed the light of reason on the human mind, God cannot deny himself, nor can truth ever contradict truth."

Faith and science work together to reveal the wonders of God, not in opposition to each another

Nowadays some people put aside their belief in God because they "believe in science." When they use the word *science*, what these people often mean is that they believe in what they can experience with their senses: what they can see, hear, and touch. They believe in what can be "proven." Because we can't see God with our eyes or prove his existence in material terms, some people reject the reality of his existence.

This doesn't make a lot of sense. After all, we believe in lots of things we can't see, such as the law of gravity, or that can't be proven, such as the love of a parent for his or her child. In other words, when your mom or dad tells you that he or she loves you, you tend to accept that as truth, even though you have no proof of it in a scientific sense. "But they take care of me, they hug me, they actually tell me they love me," you might say. This is evidence, for sure, but it's not scientific proof. Still, we trust this *evidence* because it makes sense to believe it. Sometimes we're wrong, but generally speaking, evidence gives us reason to believe.

Evidence for God's existence is not scientific like the evidence we have for the physical world. However, there is ample evidence of God's existence—so much so that it makes much more sense to believe in God than to disbelieve. Despite this, though, some people still think that "being religious" or having faith somehow can't exist alongside an acceptance of science. We also should remember that the knowledge that science uncovers often changes over the course of history, and that what scientists "knew" in one age has at times been overturned by a new generation of scientists. What persists over time is not scientific facts, but scientific *method*.

The last three popes have explicitly stated that faith and science go together. In a letter to the director of the Vatican Observatory, Pope Saint John Paul II said, "Science can purify religion from error and superstition; religion can purify science from idolatry and false absolutes. Each can draw the other into a wider world, a world in which both can flourish." Pope John Paul II is saying that faith and science must work together, because neither is able to give us a full picture of what God has done without the other. Only by having faith and using science can we begin to understand God and his works.

Speaking about the patron saint of scientists, Pope Benedict XVI said, "Saint Albert the Great reminds us that there is friendship between science and faith and that through their vocation to the study of nature,

Saint Albert the Great

scientists can take an authentic and fascinating path of holiness" (General Audience, March 24, 2010). Both science and faith study the nature of the universe. The more we know about the universe, the easier it is to know God, to love God, and to serve him.

Recently, Pope Francis said, "There cannot and must not be any opposition between faith and science." The message is very clear here: Our faith in Christ and our trust in science should work together to guide us in understanding the world around us, and should not to be in conflict with each other ("Science for Peace," July 2-3, 2000).

If you take a moment to think about it, this has to make perfect sense: Our faith tells us that God created the universe. "Science" is part of the universe; therefore, God created science. What we learn about God from our faith and what we learn about the world from science come from the same source of truth: God himself.

Pope Benedict XVI

Pope Francis

By studying science, we come to a better knowledge and understanding of God's creation. By studying our faith, we come to understand the meaning and purpose of what God created. As creatures made to be like God, we are called to really think about, pray about, and engage with the world around us in a truthful way. Without faith, science is just a cold, simplistic picture of a much bigger and more beautiful work given to us by our heavenly Father. Sure, we can know that the nearest star to ours is *Proxima Centauri*, four light-years away, but why should we care? Why does it matter?

It matters because that star demonstrates that there is a loving Artist who put the stars in the sky and, even with such a glorious tapestry of millions of stars, this same Artist lovingly made each of us so that we could appreciate the stars and all the gifts of his creation.

What is one way the link between faith and science matters in your life?

____

____

____

____

SUMMARY

- We all believe in things that can't be seen or proven by science.
- Science isn't in conflict with faith and can't replace faith because they each help us to know different things.
- Science without faith fails to help us understand the meaning of the world around us.
- Science with faith can give us the language to appreciate and understand God and his wondrous works.

THE MEANING OF SEXUALITY

CCC, 2332: "*Sexuality* affects all aspects of the human person in the unity of his body and soul. It especially concerns affectivity, the capacity to love and to procreate, and in a more general way the aptitude for forming bonds of communion with others."

Sexuality is a gift from God that enables us to love as he loves

There probably isn't any topic in the Church today that raises more questions, especially among young people, than the relationship between sex and our faith. Much like the issue of faith and science, many people today would like to believe that the subjects of faith and sex have little to do with each other. In fact, the opposite is true.

We live in a world in which a lot of people think a lot about sex a lot of the time. Sexual content and conversations appear in our social media feeds, our music, our streaming entertainment, and our advertising. Even if we didn't want to think about sex, it seems that it's never too far away. Some people even say we've never lived in a more sexualized culture than the one we're in right now.

While there are some ways in which that is certainly true—for example, it is far easier to find sexual content and conversations than ever before—it also has to be stated that human beings have always thought about sex, all throughout history. Sex wasn't suddenly discovered 50 years ago! We have loads of examples of art featuring sexual content, historical records talking about sexual activity, and laws dealing with all sorts of sexual issues, going back thousands of years.

The Birth of Venus, Boticelli

Why do people spend so much time thinking and talking about sex? The answers may seem obvious to us, but what we have to think about is the more important answer behind the easy answers: sexuality, the fact that we are male and female, and our ability to engage in sexual activity are very important gifts from God.

We know that God made us in his own image. Part of what that means is that our bodies themselves reveal how we are to love, and these bodies are formed in a way that allows us to participate in God's creative power and bring forth new human life. Think about that: God shares with us his creative power, enabling us to bring forth his most important creation: human life, the most important part of the whole universe!

The special expression of love that belongs to men and women in the relationship we call marriage is the place where families are born. Husbands and wives love one another so much that sometimes that love overflows into new life. Their children are actually the personified love they share with each other! Married love isn't just about having children, though. Married love is also about supporting each other, affirming each other, and helping each other grow in holiness. God acts through the couple; thus, they don't only love each other better, but they also love everyone else better. Their love doesn't turn them inward toward each other; it faces outward so they can share it with the world.

Sex isn't just about baby-making, though. In fact, that's only one small part of the meaning of the word *sex*. More than just actions, sex is about the way that we relate to others—not just in romantic relationships, but in all our relationships. We are friends and family and loved ones as men and women. Specifically as men and women, we bring gifts to those relationships to make them richer and more life-affirming.

List some gifts God has given you.

____

____

____

____

Thus, sexuality is about our very identity as men and women loved into existence by God. God made each one of us to fulfill a role in his plan of salvation. Each one of us has a unique, irreplaceable place in human history; we can only fulfill that role by being the best man or woman that God has made us to be.

SUMMARY

- Sex is a gift from God; therefore, our faith should inform how we think about sex.
- Being men and women allows us to share in God's creative power through the bringing forth of new life.
- Sexuality is about more than just certain kinds of actions; sexuality is about being men and women, possessing special gifts specifically as men and women.
- Our sexuality is the basis for our identity as people loved into existence by God to fulfill our role in his plan of salvation.

CCC, 1643: "Conjugal love involves a totality, in which all the elements of the person enter.... It aims at a deeply personal unity, a unity that, beyond union in one flesh, leads to forming one heart and soul."

What it means to be a man or a woman

Right at the beginning of Saint John Paul II's time as pope, he gave a series of Wednesday audiences at the Vatican organized around the theme of the meaning of our bodies. He delivered these addresses over the course of about four years. We now call this collection of teachings the "Theology of the Body." While these teaching are often very deep and challenging to understand, we can focus on some important points he shares that tell us why God made us the way he did, especially in regard to being men and women.

John Paul II begins his teaching with Jesus' invitation to reflect on how things were between men and women "from the beginning" (see Matthew 19:1–12). That invitation leads us back to thinking about the first man and woman way back in Genesis 2 and 3. In the account of the Garden of Eden, we learn why God created us the way he did and how men and women are made to be in relationship with each other. The Scripture account teaches us that being men and women is not just a biological fact; it actually reveals God's plan for us as human beings made in his image. What we're going to see as we continue to look at the Scripture account is that we are literally made for one another!

In the beginning of the Scripture about the Garden of Eden in Genesis 2, we see that God first forms a human creature out of the mud of the earth (Genesis 2:7). Our English Bible translations usually call this creature "the man," but for now, let's think of this creature as just "the human" instead. God forms a body for this human out of the earth itself. This means we are physical, material, we exist in time and space—unlike God. But then God breathes his spirit into the creature, and only then does the text say that the human is "alive." Though the creature was obviously alive before, now it is not only a physical creature; it is also a spiritual creature. Now the creature is God-like, even though it exists in a different way—that is, with a physical body.

Pope Saint John Paul II

This creature now lives at peace in the world. Because sin hadn't entered the world yet, the human had no concept of fear, didn't experience pain, and was happy. The human lived in *original innocence*. Original innocence will change after *original sin* enters the world, but we're not there yet.

Saint John Paul II continues his reflections on Genesis 2 with three "original experiences" the creature has in its innocence. The first is the experience of "original solitude." This human is alone in the garden, and God points out that the creature is not meant to be alone (see Genesis 2:18). This human understood loneliness—wanting to be seen, understood, and loved by someone else. God makes the animals for the human, but none of them is "suited" as a companion; none of them is God-like in the way that the human is.

In response to this solitude, God takes a rib from the human and forms another human out of the earth, just like the first one. Now there are two humans, two God-like beings in the garden. But there's a big difference between them. They are both embodied persons, but now there are two different ways of expressing this embodiment: they are a man and a woman. The first human, the man, exclaims his delight in seeing another creature like himself, an answer to his solitude (see Genesis 2:23). The new creature is like him, but with a body that goes together with and complements his. John Paul II calls this the "original unity of man and woman."

Finally, Genesis 2:25 tells us the man and the woman (his wife, the text says) were both naked but they felt no shame. This is the experience of "original nakedness." It's normal for us to cover ourselves when we are naked. We keep our bodies private from the eyes of others because nakedness makes us feel vulnerable. We fear that someone could hurt us, or judge us, or make fun of us, or use us. In the Garden of Eden, though, the first humans didn't have that fear. That fear was not God's design for man and woman.

Genesis 2 thus reveals that God made us men and women, two different God-like ways of being a body. Men and women have bodies that are meant to go together in a relationship where they know, respect, and trust each other because they were made to complement each other for life. We come to know what it means to be a man or a woman by realizing the ways in which we are different from one another and appreciating and thanking God for those differences.

Sadly, this all falls apart in Genesis 3. The devil tempts the man and the woman with the promise that if they eat from the tree God forbid them to eat from, they will "be like gods" (Genesis 3:5). That's the big lie: they were already like God! The devil tempts them to rely on their own ideas about who they are. The devil invites them to define themselves apart from the way God made them. And they accept the invitation—that is, the temptation. The man and woman choose their own way, thinking they could be happier than they were in obeying God. We call this event original sin.

The consequences of the man and woman's disobedience were immediate: They realized they were naked and they hid from each other. They even tried to hide from God because they were ashamed of what they had done (see Genesis 3:7-8). When God reached out to them, instead of apologizing, they made excuses. The man blamed the woman and the woman blamed the devil! The world that God had created had been changed because

the man and woman were meant to take care of each other and the world, but instead, they chose themselves instead of the good of the other and the world. The peace that God wanted for his people was broken. From this point forward, men and women would experience difficulties in their relationship with each other. They'd even have a hard time understanding themselves. They—and we—now lived in a broken world with broken relationships. The fallout of the man and woman's choice to disobey God.

This seems like a lot of bad news, except that we have the Good News of Jesus Christ. In Jesus, God chose to become a human being like us and to offer himself selflessly for us on the Cross. His Death and Resurrection makes it possible for us to be restored to our original innocence through him. Through Christ, God's loving action in our lives—his grace—empowers us to live as he originally created us to live. His grace makes it possible for us to turn away from selfishness and fear and experience open, honest, loving, and life-giving relationships. We can have all these things if we just let God be the one who defines us instead of defining ourselves or allowing the world around us to do so.

Needless to say, there's a lot more to Saint John Paul II's Theology of the Body. His reflections on the Garden of Eden—inspired by Jesus' invitation to recall how things were "in the beginning," gives us a way to understand ourselves, our bodies, our relationships, and our role in the world. We learn that we are made as God-like creatures called to love the way God loves; that is, freely and without selfishness. We also learn that we love as men and women, each with our own special gifts and particular ways of engaging the world around us. We love through our bodies, whether through the special intimacy of sex within marriage or even through a hug or caring touch we give a friend who is hurting.

Most importantly, the Theology of the Body demonstrates that we are happiest when we live according to God's plan for us, and we are unhappy when we think our ideas are better than God's.

SUMMARY

- Pope Saint John Paul II gave us a great gift in his teaching called the Theology of the Body.
- When God first created human beings, he made us men and women: two different ways of being God-like, two different ways of being a body. Our bodies allow us to live in relationship with one another, even to the point of our bodies being capable of joining together in sexual intimacy.
- Unfortunately, because of our decision to turn away from God and to sin, we now struggle to understand ourselves and often find relationships to be difficult because of human selfishness. We are tempted to use other people and other people might use us.
- However, the free gift of God's grace makes it possible, in Christ, to live closer to the way God made us to be in the beginning.

CCC, 2333: "Everyone, man and woman, should acknowledge and accept his sexual identity. Physical, moral, and spiritual difference and complementarity are oriented toward the goods of marriage and the flourishing of family life. The harmony of . . . society depends . . . on the way in which the complementarity . . . between the sexes [is] lived out."

The importance of being a man or a woman

In the last section, we looked at Pope Saint John Paul II's exploration of the account of the Garden of Eden in the Book of Genesis. We learned that God created us specifically as men and women by his divine design. It is not something that we can take for granted, as if being man or woman were just another fact that we could use to describe ourselves, in the same way we might say we are short, or have brown eyes, or that we like one kind of music over another. Being a man or being a woman reveals important truths about our God-likeness.

It seems that "being a man" or "being a woman" today is a lot more complicated than it used to be. Sometimes we talk about the terms *man* and *woman* as just being a reference to the body parts we have. But they mean more than that. In important ways, we are men and women right down to the fabric of our DNA. This is true from the very moment of our conception

and there is absolutely nothing we can do to change the fact that we are genetically a man or a woman.

Yet the composition of our bodies and biology is not the only way we can understand ourselves. Some people make a distinction between biological sex and a concept called *gender,* which encompasses a lot more of our feelings, perceptions, self-understanding, and the way we present ourselves to others. Oftentimes, the word *gender* is not even understood as being restricted to "male" and "female," but encompasses a wide range of other possibilities invoking common ideas about both at the same time or about neither. This can be very confusing—both for people who do not understand themselves definitely as a man or as a woman but also for the people who love them and want what's best for them. People often use the term *gender identity* to refer to their self-understanding in this regard, even though they are in fact a man or a woman.

To be sure, not everyone agrees on how a man or a woman is supposed to look, or dress, or even act. Some of these qualities differ depending on time or place, and some of them differ from person to person. It would be difficult for us to present a comprehensive picture that proclaims, "This is what all women are like." We should appreciate the many different ways God has made us to be, with individual gifts and aptitudes and preferences. Even recognizing these differences, though, is it possible to get some sense of what it means that God made us specifically man or woman?

We can get one really important insight into this by reflecting on one of the most obvious differences between men and women: men can be fathers and women can be mothers. Both fathers and mothers are parents, but they are not the same. Scripture gives us images of fathers as strong protectors of the things that are most important, especially their loved ones. Likewise, Scripture gives us moving images of mothers as people capable of showing love and compassion in special ways. God may use father images for himself more often, but he also uses mother images to describe his love. These two ways of being reflect different valuable truths about God and about us. Understandably, you're probably not thinking of yourself as a father or mother right now! But we can still draw value from these images to think about how we might act in our families and with our friends.

Turning now to the idea of gender identity, let's recall that who we are as persons is visible through our bodies. Remember that we don't *have* bodies; we *are* our bodies (just as we are our souls). Simply put, this means that if my body is a "man body," then I am a man. This means that our "gender identity" should match our biology. Thus, though I may perceive myself in some different way or I might understand myself as one kind of man compared to a different image of what it means to be a man, I am definitely a man. This is how God made me, and that matters.

Even if being a man or a woman is a biological reality, why does it matter if I understand myself differently, especially if adhering to my understanding makes me feel more comfortable with myself? We will consider a more detailed response to this question in the next section, but the start of the answer is very simple: It matters because being created as a man or as a woman is true. Everybody wants to live according to the truth, even if we don't always like to admit it. When we are trying to keep up a lie, we feel anxious and tense because we don't want to get caught, or because we are not at peace with ourselves. When we lie to ourselves about a relationship we're in, we don't feel joy; we feel discomfort and sadness. When we find out a friend has lied to us, we feel pain from their betrayal. We want to live in the truth—even when we know it's going to hurt to do so.

This applies to our own self-identity, too. When we try to convince ourselves that we are something we're not, we might get away with it for a while, but sooner or later the tension of our inauthenticity makes us unhappy. Because we are unhappy, we might even try to dig into the lie further, but the truth can't stop being the truth no matter what we do. Our happiness—a peace and joy that God wants for us—comes from being who God made us to be.

Rather than struggle to construct an image of ourselves as we think we should be or as we feel we should be, or even as we would like to be, we should instead seek and pray for the grace to really and truly be ourselves—as God made us.

In the whole history of God's plan for the whole universe, only you can be you. No one else can do what God made you to do, and he made you a man or a woman so you could do it.

SUMMARY

- Being a man or woman is not only a matter of biology; it is also a part of our God-given identity for a purpose.
- *Gender identity* is a term one might use to describe their self-understanding of being a man or woman.
- While how to be a man or woman sometimes varies throughout history, God's Word consistently tells us that men are called to be fathers and women are called to be mothers. This doesn't always mean mother or father in the literal sense; rather, it speaks to different ways of taking care of others in our relationships.
- In our culture today, we sometimes think of "gender identity" as something independent of biology, but a truthful understanding of ourselves can only occur when our self-understanding of who we are as either a man or a woman matches our biology.
- We can only be happy when we are truthfully ourselves and we can only fulfill God's plan for our lives when we live truthfully.

TRANSGENDER EXPERIENCES

CCC, 369: "'Being man' or 'being woman' is a reality which is good and willed by God: man and woman possess an inalienable dignity which comes to them immediately from God their Creator. . . In their 'being-man' and 'being-woman,' they reflect the Creator's wisdom and goodness."

Living the truth amidst changing cultural ideas

Because we are currently experiencing new attitudes about the most basic meanings of being man or woman, we are also seeing rapid changes in the ways in which people—especially young people such as yourself—understand themselves. In the past few years, more and more people have come to understand themselves as the opposite sex of their body or as being in some way different from any "typical" understanding of being a man or a woman, including the possibility of understanding themselves as both or neither. Furthermore, these self-understandings may change from time to time, sometimes often. The term *transgenderism* is often used to describe these different kinds of understanding.

The term *transgenderism* suggests a change from one gender to another gender, such as a person understanding themselves as a man even though their body has female sex characteristics. However, sometimes a person doesn't feel that they've changed, or that they are only one gender expression. Because this can be complicated, it has been suggested that we simply allow people to tell us how they want to be identified, if such an identification is even necessary at all.

These experiences can be distinguished from the psychological term *gender dysphoria*. A person experiencing dysphoria has discomfort with their biological sexual identity, which may or may not include identification with a different form of gender expression. Implied in the term *dysphoria* is a desire for wholeness and peace with one's body. Some people try to find this wholeness and peace in a transgender identity—in other words, in having the body of one gender but outwardly exhibiting and identifying the characteristics of the opposite gender—while others may choose a path of reconciliation between their self-understanding and their body by seeking social and physical changes.

The number of young people who have embraced a transgender identity speaks loudly to the reality that many people are uncomfortable with themselves in the world today. The reasons are easy to see: We don't always understand what a man or a woman is "supposed" to be, or if that's even a valid expectation—

though, as stated in the last section, most of us do feel that there is a way that men and women are supposed to be, even if we disagree on what that means. Sometimes painful experiences make relating to one's body uncomfortable or stressful. When someone feels that the expectations of identifying with their body are too confusing, difficult, or even frightening, self-identifying as something else might seem like the answer.

This is not to say that one "chooses" their identity. Some people talk as if they have "discovered" a transgender identity rather than having chosen anything. They also speak about the sense of peace and joy that comes from self-acceptance and finding what they believe is their "true self." However, here we run into a difficulty. We learned in previous sections that God made us—body and spirit—in his image. Our unique identity, given to us by God from the moment of our conception and never to be repeated again in the history of the universe, includes being distinctly man or woman. This God-given identity is a gift. It is an invitation to engage the world around us and the people around us so that others can come to know God's love through us. To understand our identity as different from our bodies, or as entirely fluid depending on the day, or the circumstances, or the people around us, is to suggest that we understand ourselves better than our Creator and that our ways are better than his ways.

Write a short prayer thanking God for giving you life.

____

____

____

Thus, the teaching of the Church has always been that "I"—the "real me" who I understand myself to be—is a man or a woman because my body is a man-body or a woman-body. There isn't another way to understand myself and I cannot change myself. Trying to live otherwise is a rejection of God's great gift to me.

Most people who experience a transgender identity aren't consciously rejecting God. Many struggle to find peace in themselves and their relationship with God, and the difficulty they experience leads them to the conclusion that this self-defined identity will help them find a place in the world. Adopting a transgender identity, especially in our culture right now, can lead those who feel uncomfortable, lonely, or lost to seek out a new community that affirms and supports them. Transgenderism has become such a commonplace topic today because there is a large community—especially online—that has come together as a result of the shared discomfort many people experience. For

those who are uncomfortable with themselves, finding other people with similar difficulties can be very attractive, as can becoming part of a community that affirms their false vision of themselves rather than helps them to seek the truth.

Saint Paul says, "[love] rejoices with the truth" (1 Corinthians 13:6). Despite the affirmation one may receive, transgender identities are not truthful identities. The love a person experiences is affection for a false image of the real person made in God's image. The satisfaction one finds in a transgender identity can only be temporary because it does not abide in the truth.

Helping someone struggling with transgenderism come to understand and experience the beauty and wonder of who God made them to be is a loving path. God can heal us of the pain we've experienced in our lives if we only make the choice to present ourselves to him and let his love satisfy us in ways that no other person and no other self-understanding can do.

People who have never struggled with questions of gender identity can sometimes be frustrated or uncomfortable with those who have. A lack of understanding can lead to too-easy conclusions that people just have to "get over themselves" or "deal with it." This is not a loving Christian response. Not only do all people possess dignity as children of God; Christ calls us to walk with those who are suffering, to bring his healing presence to those around us by allowing his love to shine through us. This might mean that we have to face our own discomfort, ask God to heal us, and pray that we can be more like Christ.

Only a truthful account of ourselves can ultimately bring us joy in this life and into eternity. God loves us even in the midst of our pain and discomfort and wants to heal us, but we have to let him do so.

SUMMARY

- *Transgenderism* is a term used for many different ways of understanding oneself where there is a disconnection between one's biological sex and the way the person understands himself or herself.
- In the complexity of our modern world, more young people than ever experience express discomfort in their own bodies.
- God made our bodies male or female. This is not only a biological fact; it is a statement of who we are as persons.
- We can only really love ourselves and others when we love according to the truth, which comes from God.
- We are called to have compassion and respect for all people, even when others' self-expression might make us uncomfortable.

SAME SEX ATTRACTION

CCC, 2358: "The number of men and women who have deep-seated homosexual tendencies is not negligible. This inclination, which is objectively disordered, constitutes for most of them a trial. They must be accepted with respect, compassion, and sensitivity."

We are more than what we desire

Sexual attraction is not the same thing as sexual identity. While much of this booklet has dealt with issues of how we understand ourselves as persons, this last section deals with how we find other persons to be sexually or romantically attractive to us. While most people find themselves attracted to the opposite sex, either male or female, some people find themselves predominately attracted to the same sex, and some people might find people of both sexes romantically or sexually attractive at different times in their lives.

Note that most people "find themselves" attracted to certain people. Attraction is usually not a choice; it is something that we come to realize. Nor is it something that can be easily changed, if at all. But attraction is also not a defining characteristic of a person. It is one attraction among many attractions that every person possesses as a human being. Some people prefer rap music to country music. Some people prefer chocolate ice cream over vanilla ice cream. Some people like soccer over basketball. However, even if any of these things were very important to you, you wouldn't define yourself by these attractions. You are more than a rap fan or a chocolate ice cream eater or a soccer player or fan.

The same thing applies to our romantic and sexual attractions. While our relationships with other people are certainly some of the most important parts of our lives, we should never be defined by our relationship with another person. The only relationship that should define our identity is our relationship with Christ. We enter into sexual relationships with the opposite sex in marriage because marriage is a gift to us from God that enables a man and a woman to be a living symbol of his love and self-giving in Christ.

When a person experiences romantic or sexual attraction to a person or persons of the same sex, there is nothing moral or immoral about the attraction itself. It is just an attraction. Because we have the gift of freedom given to us by God, we get to decide how we *respond* to each of our attractions. When we are attracted to something good, like helping someone who is struggling, then we can say this attraction is *ordered* toward what is good. However, when we are attracted to something that is not in line with God's law revealed in God's created order in nature, we call this a *disordered* attraction. Because of human sinfulness, we all experience disordered attractions that pull us toward choices that are not good for us and that lead us away from happiness here and in eternity. Thus, we have to pray to cooperate with God's grace—his constant love for us—so we can choose to do what is moral and good and refuse to do what is not morally good.

Our sexuality—both the fact that we are man-bodies and woman-bodies and also the fact that our bodies can be joined sexually—is a great gift empowering us to share in God's love and creative power in the marriage of man and woman. Sex in marriage (the "marital act") becomes a symbol of God's love in the joining of the spouses' bodies in joy. This is especially so when their love overflows into the conception of their child. This is the God-given meaning of sexual intercourse.

List three choices that cooperate with God's grace.

1.____________________________

2.____________________________

3.____________________________

List three that do not.

1.____________________________

2.____________________________

3.____________________________

Sexual activity between two people of the same sex—whether physical activity or in fantasies—becomes just a false attempt to do or think about something with the same meaning God inscribed in our bodies. These false attempts may be acts that convey sincere affection, maybe even a desire for the good of the other, but they can't be holy acts or moral acts because the very meaning of the act given to us by God can't be realized by two men or two women.

Does this mean that people who only feel attracted to the same sex can never experience love, sex, or marriage? Not exactly. While sex is reserved for marriage and marriage is only between a man and a woman, all people are called to love and be loved. Though our world makes it hard to believe, love and sex are not the same thing and no one actually *needs* sex to survive...or even to be happy in life. All people—married and unmarried—are called to *chastity*. Chastity is related to temperance, or self-control. When we live out the virtue of chastity, we regulate our sexual activity in accord with our state in life. When we are chaste, we don't find sexual attractions to be a burden or something to obsess over. Our attention is focused properly on our relationship with Christ *first*, with all other relationships coming after that. Persons with predominant attractions to the same sex are called to refrain from sexual love, but not from love, intimacy, and friendship in non-sexual ways, and they are empowered to do so when they put Christ first.

SUMMARY

- Every person has a variety of attractions. While some attractions are more powerful or more significant than others, the only "attraction" that should define who we are as persons is our relationship with Christ.
- Some attractions are ordered to morally good acts and some are disordered and draw us toward immoral acts. We possess the freedom to choose between moral and immoral actions. When we ask Christ for help in choosing, he makes it easier for us to choose the good.
- Marriage between a man and a woman is a symbol of Christ's love for the Church and sex within marriage is a sharing in God's ability to create. Because of this, any sexual activity or thoughts about sexual activity outside of marriage are disordered.
- All people are called to be chaste. Therefore, people who experience predominant attraction to only the same sex should focus on building strong and joyful non-sexual friendships.

RESOURCES

For further reading on the topics discussed in this book, we recommend exploring the following official resources from the Vatican and the United States Conference of Catholic Bishops (USCCB).

Dignitas Infinita (Infinite Dignity) :

press.vatican.va/content/salastampa/en/bollettino/pubblico/2024/04/08/240408c.html

Male and Female He Created Them:

https://www.vatican.va/roman_curia/congregations/ccatheduc/documents/rc_con_ccatheduc_doc_20190202_maschio-e-femmina_en.pdf

USCCB Teaching Resources:

www.usccb.org/resources/gender-ideology-select-teaching-resources

Pastoral Letter: "On the Unity of the Body and Soul" by Archbishop Paul Coakley

https://archokc.org/pastoral-letters

Prayer to Mary, Mother of the Church

Mother, help our faith!

Open our ears to hear God's Word and to recognize his voice and call.

Awaken in us a desire to follow in his footsteps, to go forth from our own land and to receive his promise.

Help us to be touched by his love, that we may touch him in faith.

Help us to entrust ourselves fully to him and to believe in his love, especially at times of trial, beneath the shadow of the Cross, when our faith is called to mature.

Sow in our faith the joy of the Risen One.

Remind us that those who believe are never alone.

Teach us to see all things with the eyes of Jesus, that he may be light for our path. And may this light of faith always increase in us, until the dawn of that undying day, which is Christ himself, your Son, our Lord! Amen.

(Pope Francis, Encyclical Letter, Lumen Fidei)

Vatican Gardens, Mater Ecclesiae Monastery